MORE

CHURCH
CHUCKLES

MORE CHURCH CHUCKLES

by DICK HAFER

New Leaf Press

First printing: October 1995
Second printing: April 1996

Copyright © 1995 by New Leaf Press. All rights reserved. Printed in the United States of America. No part of this book may be used or reproduced in any manner whatsoever without written permission of the publisher except in the case of brief quotations in articles and reviews. For information write: New Leaf Press, Inc., P.O. Box 311, Green Forest, AR 72638.

ISBN: 0-89221-305-1
Library of Congress Catalog: 95-71122

Please feel free to use these pages for your bulletins, fax messages, etc.

Dedication

To my wife of 37 years, Mary, who
serves as my co-idea generator, loving
editor, and critic-in-residence.

These cartoons are not meant to make fun
of God's _church_ but to get us to laugh with each other
at the ways of God's _people_ . . . us.

The most effective ministers I've ever known
all shared a vibrant sense of humor.

After all, who has more to be happy about than us?
I've read the back of the book . . . we win!

With the fearful strain that is on me night and day,
if I did not laugh I should die. — *Abraham Lincoln (1809-1865)*

Laughter adds richness, texture, and color to otherwise ordinary days.
It is a gift, a choice, a discipline, and an art. — *Tim Hansel*

ENJOY THAT LATE MOVIE ON TV LAST NIGHT, "MR. HOT SHOT TEACHER"?

WELL . . . HELLO THERE, PASTOR . . . THAT SURE WAS A FUNNY DENTIST JOKE
IN YOUR SERMON LAST SUNDAY.

THE MORNING THE UNEXPECTED GUEST PREACHER ARRIVED.

I WON'T BE TALKIN' TOO MUCH IN CLASS TODAY, MR. JENKINS. . . . I'VE GOT THE FLU.

OH NO YOU DON'T! **OUR** CHRISTMAS CAROLING TEAM IS GOING TO DEAR, SWEET OLD WIDOW EVANS'.... WHO GIVES OUT GREAT BROWNIES AND HOT CHOCOLATE!

SHE'S BEEN LIKE THAT EVER SINCE THE NEW, CUTE, SINGLE YOUTH MINISTER ARRIVED.

REALLY?!! ... YOU'VE BEEN A MEMBER HERE FOR SIX YEARS? ... HOW ABOUT THAT?

IT DOESN'T SAY WHAT TIME THE SERVICES ARE.

WHERE DID THAT **FIFTY** GO THAT WAS IN HERE?... **WAIT! OH, NO!!**

THE NEW YOUTH PASTOR IS STILL A LITTLE BIT NERVOUS.

A PARTICULARLY BAD EASTER SUNDAY MORNING IN THE CHOIR REHEARSAL ROOM.

dich hafer

I'VE COME FOR CONFESSION. DO YOU HAVE A FEW HOURS?

OOH!...HE LOOKS....JUST LIKE HIS DADDY!

IF WE WARNED HIM ONCE, WE WARNED HIM A THOUSAND TIMES...
30 MINUTES, TOPS!

IT SHOULD BE EASY FOR YOU TO FIND. . . . I LIVE IN A BIG WHITE HOUSE
WITH A BIG DOOR AND WINDOWS. . . .

WHOA!! FINISHED JUST IN TIME!

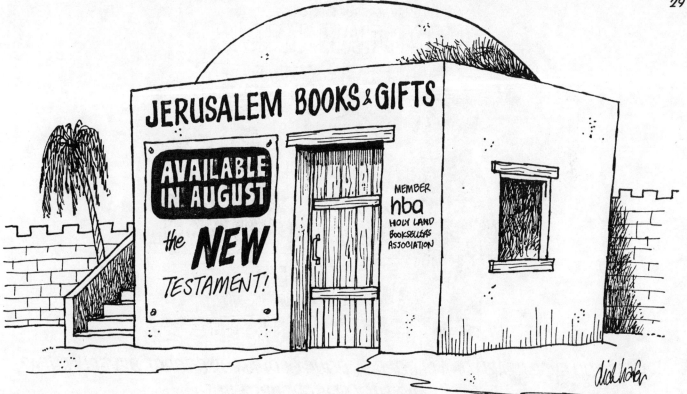

HAVE YOU EVER HEARD OF A RECORD BY DOUG OLDHAM OR GEORGE BEVERLY SHEA?
ARE THEY NEW GROUPS?

FISH AGAIN?!! *HOW ABOUT SOME BAGELS AND LOX?* **THAT'D BE A MIRACLE!!**

GOOD AFTERNOON, I AM THE EVANGELTRON 3000, FROM WHITLEY MEMORIAL AME CHURCH.... PLEASE TAKE THIS MATERIAL.... IF YOU WOULD LIKE MORE INFORMATION, PLEASE PUSH THE TOP LEFT BUTTON....

LOST
AND
FOUND

dick hofer

TRUST ME... IF YOU'D LISTEN TO THEIR RECORD **BACKWARDS** THEY SAY HORRIBLE THINGS!

THIS OUGHT TO GIVE A BIG BOOST TO OUR EVANGELISM PROGRAM, BROTHER EDWIN.
WE'RE THE FIRST CHURCH IN PLYMOUTH TO HAVE A
BRAND NEW, STATE-OF-THE-ART SOUND SYSTEM.

WHEN YOU GUYS GET THE AIR CONDITIONER FIXED . . . *THAT'S* WHEN!

DO YOU SUPPOSE IT COULD BE A SIGN?

GO **HOME?!!** ARE YOU KIDDING, GWEN?!! FOR A COUPLE OF SNOWFLAKES?

GO TO **CHURCH?!!** ARE YOU KIDDING, GWEN?!! IT'S GONNA RAIN ANY MINUTE!!

IT'S GOING PRETTY GOOD TODAY, PASTOR. WE'VE SOLD 1 OF YOUR "BEARING THE BURDEN" TAPES, 3 OF "THE CHRISTIAN'S RESPONSIBILITIES," AND 76 OF "HOW TO GET EVERYTHING YOU EVER WANTED, RIGHT NOW, THROUGH PRAYER."

OH . . . "PRAYING HANDS" . . . HOW NICE.

HERE YOU ARE, MY GOOD MAN . . . A TRACT AND A FOLDER ABOUT OUR CHURCH. WE HAVE ALL KINDS OF MINISTRIES . . . EVEN A DIET GROUP THAT MAY HELP YOU WITH THAT EXTRA WEIGHT.

ALL I SAID WAS THAT GOD IS KIND OF LIKE THEIR EARTHLY FATHER.

BUT *EVERYONE* IS GONNA GET SOME CRITICISM ONCE IN A WHILE! *NOW FOR PETE'S SAKE, COME ON OUT FROM BEHIND THERE, PASTOR!!*

HERBERT! CAN'T YOU GIVE YOUR DAUGHTER A MEASLY FIVE OR SIX HOURS OF YOUR TIME?!!

GUESS WHAT!! WHILE I WAS WAITING IN THE CAR FOR YOU AFTER CHURCH,
A NICE MAN IN THE PARKING LOT GAVE ME SEVEN **GREAT** LITTLE PUPPIES!!

SOMETIMES I REMEMBER THE NICE DAYS BEFORE WE WERE A **MEGACHURCH.**

THE EARLY CHURCH IN AMERICA.

SO I FIGURE IF WE ALL SLIP INTO THE VOTER'S MEETING QUIETLY,
WE CAN TAKE OVER THIS PLACE!

dick hafer

SO THEN WE ALL AGREE THAT OUR MAJOR SPIRITUAL GOAL FOR THE YEAR
IS TO PAVE THE PARKING LOT?

DO YOU HAVE CHANGE FOR A ONE?

BUT IT WORKED FOR MARTIN LUTHER....

KEEP OFF

GLENVILLE CHRISTIAN SCHOOL

dick hafer

PASTOR FOWLER!!?

PASTOR, SHOULDN'T WE DO SOMETHING SPIRITUAL ON
OUR CAMPING TRIP? EVERYONE COULD COME INTO MY TENT FOR
AN ALL-NIGHT PRAYER MEETING.... PLEASE?

A PICTORIAL CHURCH DIRECTORY *IS* A NICE IDEA, I AGREE ... BUT
HE'S BEEN WORKING ON IT FOR ELEVEN YEARS!

LOOK AT THAT!! THEY'RE AT IT AGAIN! LAND SAKES, THOSE BRATS OF THE PASTOR'S ARE THE MOST ILL-BEHAVED HELLIONS IN THE CHURCH! WHY ARE THE PASTOR'S CHILDREN ALWAYS THE MOST DISOBEDIENT? **LAUGHING** AND **TALKING** INSIDE THE SANCTUARY WHEN CHURCH ENDED ONLY TEN MINUTES AGO!

WELL . . . I SEE YOU'VE ALREADY MET MY MOTHER. SHE'S GOING TO BE VISITING US FOR A FEW WEEKS.

A CHILD IS SITTING IN GRANDMOTHER'S MEMORIAL PEW! GO REMOVE HIM!

WAIT A MINUTE....

I FEEL THAT YOUR MARITAL DIFFICULTIES MIGHT BE RESOLVED IF YOU USED A LITTLE MORE TACT, BIGMOUTH!

"I SEE . . . YES . . . I AGREE . . . YOU'RE RIGHT, AS USUALL . . . MMMM . . . OH, YES . . . THAT THRILLS MY HEART . . . RIGHT . . . UH HUH . . . WHATEVER YOU SAY. . . ."

BOY! HE'S REALLY HAD IT TOUGH! SOMEBODY OUGHT TO
WRITE A BOOK ABOUT HIS PROBLEMS!

SO, IT'S WITH A HEAVY HEART THAT I LEAVE MY FLOCK BEHIND FOR A VACATION.

"SELL WHAT YOU HAVE!"... "GIVE THE MONEY TO THE POOR!"... BOY, HE'S GOT A LOT TO LEARN ABOUT STARTING A RELIGION!!

ANOTHER ONE! IF THIS KEEPS UP, THE CAPERNAUM HOSPITAL-DRIVE IS DOWN THE TUBES!

YEAH, PASTOR, WE'VE BEEN CHURCH SHOPPING FOR SOME TIME — BUT **THIS** POTLUCK SUPPER PUTS YOU WAY OUT IN FRONT!

WHO CHECKED HIS CREDENTIALS?

NO — NORMALLY WE **ENCOURAGE** BROWSING, BUT....

LOOK! KEN AND MARSHA ARE BRINGING THEIR QUINTUPLETS TO CHURCH FOR THE FIRST TIME!

HAVE A NICE CONGREGATIONAL BUSINESS MEETING, DEAR.

FIRST PRESBYTERIAN EVANGELISM TEAM PRACTICE.

GOOD MORNING. AH... PASTOR IS AWAY TODAY... WELL, NOT REALLY **AWAY**... HE'S OUT OF TOWN ...ACTUALLY, I GUESS THAT IS AWAY... HE'LL BE BACK ON TUESDAY, OR SOME TIME... I GUESS... AH... HE ASKED ME TO DELIVER THE MESSAGE THIS MORNING... AH... I HOPE YOU LIKE IT... I'M SURE IT WILL THRILL YOUR HEART... I'M CERTAINLY... AH... EXCITED BY IT....

WHICH CLASS HAS THE MOST PRETTY GIRLS?... IN A SPIRITUAL SENSE, OF COURSE!

WELCOME TO THE CHURCH AT GLEN OAK WOODS. SUNDAY GATHERING BEGINS IN 15 MINUTES. YOU MIGHT ENJOY "PROSPERITY — RIGHT NOW!" IN ROOM 26, OR "SPIRITUAL THEMES DELVED FROM NINJA FILMS" IN THE PARLOR, OR "SING ALONG WITH RENALDO" IN THE CLUB ROOM.

81

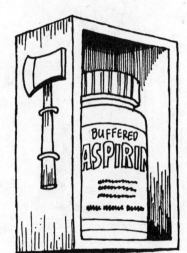

I'M SURE WE ALL WANT TO THANK MY WIFE FOR ANOTHER LOVELY SOLO.

HELLO UP THERE, PASTOR!...I FOUND THE PROBLEM!...THE
ROPE WAS CAUGHT!...I FIXED IT!!

REALLY, GUYS... I'M SORRY, BUT AFTER A COUPLE OF MONTHS IN THIS GROUP, I'VE JUST DEVELOPED TOO MUCH SELF-ESTEEM TO BE SEEN MEETING WITH MESSED-UP FOLKS LIKE YOU.

WELL, WE WILL CONSIDER YOU, PASTOR OSGOOD... BUT WE HAD
PLANNED ON SOMEONE MORE... ER... "CONVENTIONAL."

THE NEW YOUTH MINISTER IS TRYING HARD TO BE "ONE OF THE GANG."

MOMMY!...WHERE'S RUDOLPH?...AND FROSTY?...AND DONNER AND BLITZEN?
WHAT KIND OF CHRISTMAS IS THIS?

FIRST BAPTIST HAD 1,786 IN SUNDAY SCHOOL LAST WEEK.

BECAUSE WE DON'T THINK BILLY GRAHAM WOULD ACCEPT A CALL TO POSSUM CORNERS BAPTIST CHURCH! . . . *THAT'S* WHY!! NOW SHUT UP, HAZEL!

SO WE YOUTH GROUP LEADERS HAVE DECIDED THAT YOU CANNOT HOLD HANDS ON CHURCH PROPERTY, THAT BOYS AND GIRLS CAN'T PHONE EACH OTHER, ALL CONVERSATIONS MUST BE ABOUT SPIRITUAL MATTERS, AND DATING IS DISCOURAGED. AFTER ALL, WE YOUNG GIRLS CAN'T BE TOO CAREFUL!

MRS. BLOOMHAGEN DOESN'T UNDERSTAND WHY SHE
CAN'T SAVE A FEW SEATS FOR THE CANTATA.

THIS YEAR THE CHURCH HIRED AN OUTSIDE TEAM
TO HANDLE THE ANNUAL STEWARDSHIP DRIVE.

MOM!!

I'M SURE IT WOULD MAKE YOUR LIFE EASIER... BUT I SIMPLY CAN'T PREACH
THAT KIDS WHO EAT THEIR BEETS ARE GUARANTEED TO GO TO HEAVEN!

DOES THIS MEAN YOU'RE **NOT** INTERESTED IN VISITING OUR CHURCH?

BUT WE THOUGHT YOU'D LIKE IT. THE YOUTH PASTOR'S CAR
OUGHT TO REFLECT A SORT OF HIP SPIRITUALITY.

OK!!... WHO'S BEEN FOOLIN' WITH THE VCR?!!

WAIT A MINUTE! HOW DID **THIS** GET IN HERE? IT WAS PUBLISHED **AFTER** 1915!

WAIT A MINUTE!! *WHO GAVE THE DRIVER HIS INSTRUCTIONS?!!*

NO!! I SAID, "THROW THOSE OLD **TILES** AWAY"!!

HELLO, I'M LAMAR W. LUNDY... I'M A VOLUNTEER WITH THE PRISON MINISTRY... I'M HERE TO WITNESS TO YOU FELLOWS... I'M KIND OF NEW... I'M GOING TO BE SICK....

HERE YOU ARE, MARSHA DEAR. IT'S SO WONDERFUL TO BE ABLE TO HELP THE LESS
FORTUNATE IN A CONCRETE WAY. I'VE BROUGHT THREE SCRUMPTIOUS BALL GOWNS,
SEVERAL SHEER NEGLIGEES, A FORMAL PANTSUIT, SOME HIGH-HEELED GUCCI SHOES. . . .

OH DEAR . . . I'M AFRAID MY GUIDE DOG LICKED SOMEONE'S FOOT AGAIN.

I'D LIKE TO THANK THE CONGREGATION FOR THEIR CONCERN WHILE MY WIFE'S BEEN OUT OF TOWN WITH HER SICK MOTHER.

I'LL VOLUNTEER TO EVANGELIZE THE FOOTBALL TEAM!!

BERNIE, I WENT ALONG WITH THE "BLESSING OF THE PETS" SERVICE... BUT THE "BLESSING OF THE PERSONAL COMPUTERS" IS JUST GOING TOO FAR!

SARAH REACHED HER TOLERANCE LIMIT WHEN DOROTHY INVOKED "ROBERTS RULES OF ORDER" FOR THE 27TH TIME AT THE LADIES' GUILD MEETING.

RIVERDALE METHODIST'S FIRST ATTEMPT AT A "SMALL GROUP" MINISTRY.

OH, ISN'T THAT **CUTE**, PASTOR?! REX USUALLY TAKES
QUITE A WHILE TO WARM UP TO VISITORS!

YOU CAN'T EVER **REALLY** UNWIND, CAN YOU, HERMAN?

"DONATION" OR NOT ... IT MUST MATCH THE OTHERS!

SEE... THE CHURCH BUDGET WON'T ALLOW FOR NEW ROBES.
FOR A FEW MONTHS YOU CAN USE OUR PREVIOUS PASTOR'S ROBES.

ADAM AND EVE'S FIRST ARGUMENT

YOU'RE JUST LIKE YOUR MOTHER!!
...OH...SCRATCH THAT LAST REMARK.

NURSERY

AGES 1-3

NOW I KNOW WHY THEY'RE CALLED CHURCH "BORED" MEETINGS!

138 CABLE CHANNELS...AND THE ONLY RELIGIOUS PROGRAMMING IS ON FROM 3 TO 4:30 A.M.!

AFTER 14 MONTHS OF PREPARATION, THE MISSIONARY FINALLY MAKES IT INTO THE DEEPEST JUNGLE VILLAGE, WHERE CIVILIZED MAN HAS NEVER BEEN ENCOUNTERED.

THE USHERS WILL NOW COME FORWARD TO TAKE UP A SPECIAL EMERGENCY COLLECTION, TO HELP PAY OUR PAST-DUE ELECTRIC BILL.

THEY SENT US THIS NEW TRANSLATION OF THE BIBLE. THE "SCHOLARS" HAVE CUT OUT ALL OF THE PARTS THEY DECLARED UNTRUE.

Coming soon . . .

. . . from your favorite Christian bookstore or call